PRE/ PEA RIVER:
LIVING IN LIGHT OF ETERNITY

By Dr. Allen Baker

Table of Contents

What could be better than heaven? What could be
worse than hell? Many Christians, if not most, think
people's eternal destinations are either heaven or
hell. The Bible, however, teaches something quite
different. Heaven and hell are but intermediate states
for believers and non-believers, respectively.
Something far more glorious awaits believers who are
found in Christ – the new heavens and new earth –
and something far more dreadful awaits unbelievers
who fail to repent and believe – the lake of fire. In
these sermons, Al Baker candidly and vividly paints a
picture of eternity. His accessible language and
sound biblical instruction will convict people of their
sin, convince them of their need for Christ, and offer
unshakeable hope for all who take hold of God's
promises by faith.

So many who heard the sermons, both members of
Pea River Church and visitors, still remember them
well. Rev. Baker truly challenged and helped to
reshape their perspectives on life after death, and the
passion with which he preached left an indelible
impression upon those who were present. They
realized their sentiments about loved ones who have
died in Christ, though well-intentioned, did not fully
capture what it means to be in God's presence and to
move from glory to glory. They realized that their
fears about hell, though great, did not fully capture
what it means to live outside God's presence and to
move from torment to torment. Perhaps the most
lasting lesson was the need for each person to reflect
upon eternity. What a permanent encouragement
eternity provides for all who are found in Christ and
what a pressing warning eternity provides for those
who have failed to repent and believe! May God use

these sermons to encourage and convict all who read
them as he continues to build his kingdom.

Reverend Brewer Ames
Pastor
Pea River Presbyterian Church
Clio, Alabama

Foreword

What follows in this book are sermons I preached in July, 2017 at the Pea River Presbyterian Church, Clio, Alabama. In the 1820's, prior to the Creek Indian cession (giving up their rights to land), Scot immigrants from Richmond County, North Carolina settled in what is now Barbour County. The Pea River Presbyterian Church was established in 1823 when fifteen Scottish immigrants from Richmond County, North Carolina signed a church charter.

The Session minutes from April 17, 1879, apparently in an effort to raise money to improve the church building, write, "A few years ago our fathers assembled here regularly to worship God and to glorify the Savior's name. Here a large majority of us were, in our infancy, dedicated by our parents to God in the scared ordinance of Baptism; and here in like manner, many of us have dedicated our little children. And if we know anything of the Savior's love, it was in this house the most of us learned it. It is in this holy sanctuary of God that we have been taught the words of eternal life, and learned the way of salvation through a crucified Redeemer. It is here, we trust, that through the influence of God's word and Spirit, we were led to repentance toward God, and faith in our Lord Jesus Christ. And it is here that we devoutly hope and pray that, through God's ordained means of grace, which shall be here dispensed, that our children and friends and neighbors, and generations yet to follow us, shall be holy and saved, and brought to the knowledge of truth, as revealed in the Holy Scriptures. . . for to us, there is no other place under heaven, surrounded by so many sacred memories and hallowed association. Then in view of all these things, shall we, for want of a few dollars, suffer this church, the church of our fathers and mothers, this church hallowed to us by so many sacred memories to go down? God forbid; and let all the people say amen."

So the Pea River Presbyterian Church of Clio, Alabama has had a long and faithful history of service to our Lord Jesus Christ. I found it a great joy to preach the gospel to the saints at Pea River Presbyterian Church and what follows are those four sermons I preached to them in July, 2017.

I preach without notes but what follows is generally what I preached on those four nights. I developed what follows from a basic outline I used in preparing to preach these sermons. The thrust of these sermons is two-fold. On the one hand I hope to comfort the afflicted, but on the other hand, I hope to afflict the comfortable. America has never been more religious than today. I did not say that we are more Christian for that is obviously not true. However we are very religious and spiritual. I find this especially true in the Southeast United States where a majority of people still claim to be Christians and confess to a general Christian ethic. However as we dig more deeply into the personal lives of many professing Christians we find that they hold to a form of godliness but seem to lack the power of it. Christians divorce as much as non-Christians. Christian men are as addicted to pornography as non-Christian men. Dishonest business practices are just as prevalent with church officers as with officers of any secular club in town. Just as many Christians are seen taking their children to play travel ball on Sundays as non-

Christians. And just as many professing Christians have abortions as pagans do. I could go on and on with this line of reasoning, but surely you can see my concern.

So my prayer is that God will use these sermons to strike godly fear in the lives of comfortable, professing Christians who are living contrary to God's word, that they will see they are in danger of hell fire, even though they profess faith in Jesus Christ. But my prayer is also for true believers who are grieving the loss of a Christian loved one, or who are facing an uncertain future with a recently diagnosed disease. They surely believe their loved one is in heaven, but they want to know more about what heaven is like, what their loved one is doing there. And they want to have some assurance and comfort as their own death may be imminent. More specifically, they want to know, as far as Scripture allows us to know, exactly what happens the moment a Christian dies.

We all know that we are going to die one day. None of us like much to think about this, but we know it is true, nonetheless. We also know, though some are trying very hard to discount or deny it, that when we die we all will stand before God and give account of our lives. Hebrews 9:27 tells us that it is appointed for men to die once, and then comes the judgment. So what follows is a clarion call to all people everywhere to live their lives in light of eternity.

This short book has a two fold message. On the one hand, my prayer is that God will use this book in your life, if you are already a Christian, to encourage you, to give you a Biblical hope for eternity, to strengthen you as you go through the many hardships of life. And on the other hand, I pray this book will find its way into the hands of people who are not yet, for whatever reason, followers of Jesus Christ. I pray the Holy Spirit will work on your heart and mind and give you a holy jealousy for what Christians look forward to in eternity; and that the Spirit will arouse in your heart a fear of what awaits you on the other side if you refuse Christ's gift of eternal life.

Theologians speak of the "intermediate state." By this they mean two things. First, it refers to what happens to Christians at death, that they gain heaven, but are waiting for the final consummation of all things, the second coming of Jesus Christ. And second, the intermediate state for unbelievers refers to what happens to them at death, that is hell, as they await the Great White Throne Judgment. And while the intermediate state for believers is very comforting and encouraging and for unbelievers it is fearful and disturbing, the intermediate state yields, in God's timing, the final state for the believer on the new earth and for unbelievers their final state in the lake of fire.

So, in what follows I hope to layout, in four chapters, what happens to believers the moment of their deaths, what happens to unbelievers the moment they draw their last breath in death, what happens to the believer in his final state, and what also happens to the unbeliever in his final and eternal state.

May God the Holy Spirit work mightily in each of you and do the work of grace which only He can do.

Heaven: What Exactly Happens the Moment a Christian Dies?

Therefore, being always of good courage, and knowing that while we are at home in the body we are absent from the Lord—for we walk by faith and not by sight—we are of good courage, I say, and prefer to be absent from the body and to be at home with the Lord. Therefore we also have as our ambition whether at home or absent, to be pleasing to Him. For we must all appear before the judgment seat of Christ, so that each one may be recompensed for his deeds in the body, according to what he has done, whether good or bad. Therefore, knowing the fear of the Lord, we persuade men, 2 Corinthians 5:6-10.

At the very moment a Christian dies, what happens? What happens to his soul? Let's imagine, for a moment, that I am your pastor. You have not been feeling well for some time, very lethargic, given to pretty wild mood swings, increasingly forgetful, and have been suffering some pretty severe headaches for the last year or so. Finally, your wife convinces you to go to your doctor for a full physical examination. He sees a few things which give him concern and he sends you to a specialist to either affirm or deny his suspicions. The specialist runs various tests and gives you the worst possible news. You have an inoperable brain tumor. He is very sorry, but there is little he can do. Chemo therapy and radiation treatments may slow down the disease, but the outcome is inevitable. You are going to die. No question about it. You have at most two years to live. You can try alternative cancer treatments, which your specialist encourages, but he is pretty steadfast. "Get your house in order. You are not long for this world."

Now as your pastor, I get the bad news from your wife and immediately sit down with you and your wife at your home. What would I say to you? After all, you profess faith in Christ. There is no reason to doubt your conversion. You have walked with Christ for many years, though you readily admit that you have never been perfect. So, what would I say to you? Here is what I would say.

I am very sad about your diagnosis, and I promise to pray daily for your healing, asking God to glorify Himself by your godly response before your family and friends in the midst of this trial. God may very well heal you, for He certainly has the power to do so. Therefore, in accordance with James 5:14,15 I suggest you call for the elders of our church to anoint you with oil and to pray for your healing. At the same time, we must also realize that His will is not always to heal, that sometimes His people die after much prayer has been given to God in heaven on their behalf. So, there are five things I want you to keep in mind as you move forward while fighting this cancer.

First, I want you to be of good courage. Trust in the Lord. Be like Job, when after all his trials he was able to say, 'Though He slay me, yet I will praise Him.' Always be rejoicing in the Lord, no matter what your lot. That is what Paul is telling the Corinthians. Yes, we grieve for those we have lost in death, but we do not grieve as those who have no hope. It is only natural to grieve for the loss of a loved one, but the Christian grieves differently from the unbeliever. They have no hope and are without God in this world, but you have One who sticks closer than a brother, One who will never leave you nor forsake you, One who always lives to make intercession for you. Jesus, the Father, the Holy Spirit and angels in heaven are constantly having conversation about you. Jesus loves you and is praying moment by moment for you. How can this be? Because God has given us eternal life and this life is in His Son. He who has the Son, has the life. He who does not have the Son of God does not have the life. Paul readily admits that to be at home in the body (alive in this world, living in our physical bodies) is to be absent from the presence of the Lord in heaven. Scripture plainly proclaims that you have eternal life now, if you have the Son of God.

Secondly, I want you to live by faith and not by sight. What does this mean? You received Christ Jesus the Lord by faith at your conversion. That is, you simply believed what God says about your sinful condition before Him, and that Jesus Christ, the perfect, sinless Son of God, died for your sins and was raised to justify you before the Father. Now you are to walk by faith. He tells us that if we believe in Jesus then we have eternal life. No one can snatch you out of the Father's hand, and no one can snatch you out of your Savior's hand. No matter what happens over the next few years, please hold on to what you know to be true about God and your position before Him. There no doubt will be times of great sorrow, a great sense of loss concerning your wife, children, grandchildren, friends, and all the things you have enjoyed in this life. You probably will have bouts with anger and fear as well. You may even question God's goodness, especially when after a period of time your body seems to be rallying against the disease, that perhaps you are in remission, only to find that the cancer is

3

stronger than ever. To live by faith in this situation means to not look to your circumstances, but to the One who loves you and gave Himself for you, the One who promises that He will walk with you through the valley of the shadow of death.

Thirdly, I want you truly to believe that to be absent from the body is to be present or at home with the Lord. By this Paul means that at the moment you close your eyes in death, you will be in the presence of Jesus Christ, your Lord and Savior. Now because this is true, I want you to do everything you can, in the time you have left on this earth, to live in a way that is pleasing to the Lord. What does this mean? We all should be living this way everyday but because you know death is a real possibility, you are far more conscious of this need than others will be. Think of it like this. You can say, 'I desire more than anything God's smile on my thoughts, speech, actions, and values. I also dread more than anything His frown on my thoughts, speech, actions, and values.' I want you to say every morning to the Lord, 'Good morning Father, Son, and Holy Spirit. I dedicate myself to You today. I surrender my will totally to You today. Give me the grace to be gracious to everyone, including my wife and children. Bring to my mind those whom I have wronged over the years, and I promise to make every effort to make things right with them.'

Fourthly, why do I want you to do all you can to be of good courage, to walk by faith, and to do all you can to be pleasing to the Lord? Because you will stand before Him and be recompensed, or rewarded, for all the deeds you have done in your body, while you were living in this world, whether they were good or bad. Repentance, reconciliation, contrition, and restitution are wonderful tools God has given us to clear our consciences. So, get your house in order. Do you have anyone whom you have wronged and not yet asked for forgiveness? Are there any conversations you need to have with someone from your past? Do you need to make restitution to anyone for treating him unfairly or dishonestly? Even as a believer it is a pretty daunting thing to know that you will be judged, not for salvation in heaven or damnation in hell, for that has already been meted out on Jesus; but judged according to the rewards you will receive or be denied, based on your level of obedience. And though you will certainly know where you have failed, you nonetheless, due to your union with Christ by faith in His death and resurrection, will hear the marvelous words of hope, 'Well done, good and faithful servant.' At that point you will know without a doubt that your salvation is based solely and completely on the grace and mercy of God.

And fifthly, I urge you to use your remaining time on this earth to persuade your friends, neighbors, and family members that they too must prepare to meet God. Since everyone will stand before God and give account of their deeds, words, and thoughts, and since you are very conscience of your impending death and what follows, speak to people about their souls. Warn unbelievers to flee from the wrath of God which is coming and to believe on the Lord Jesus Christ. Encourage Christians to wait patiently and joyfully for their promotion to the presence of God in heaven.

But now, let's say that after all the cancer treatments and all the prayers, that you have just died. I gather your family together at your home after the funeral home employees have come for your body. What shall I say to them?

Here's what I would say. *I am very sorry for your loss. I am sure you are now wondering what has happened to your loved one. Because there is every evidence he was a Christian when he died, the very moment he died, four things immediately happened to him. Hebrews 12:22-24 is very instructive in this regard.*

"But you have come to Mount Zion and to the city of the Living God, the heavenly Jerusalem and to myriads of angels, to the general assembly and the church of the firstborn who are enrolled in heaven, and to God, the Judge of all, and to the spirits of the righteous made perfect, and to Jesus, the Mediator of the new covenant, and to the sprinkled blood, which speaks better than the blood of Abel."

First, the moment your loved one died he entered into perfect fellowship with the heavenly angels and all the saints of all the ages. The book of Revelation in chapter four, verse eleven, tells us that there are myriads of angels, thousands and thousands of them, twenty-four elders which are symbolic of all the leaders in the church of Jesus Christ, and four living creatures which are probably the Cherubim or Seraphim mentioned in the Old Testament. They are all giving glory to God, saying, 'Worthy art Thou, our Lord and our God, to receive glory and honor and power, for Thou hast created all things, and because of Thy will they existed and were created.'
They also are continually singing glory to Christ, 'Worthy are Thou to take the book and to break its seals, for Thou wast slain, and didst purchase for God with Thine own blood, those of every tongue, tribe,

people, and nation,' (Revelation 5:9). Myriads and myriads of angels and glorified saints, the twenty-four elders, and the four living creatures are gathered before the throne saying with a loud voice, 'Worthy is the Lamb that wast slain to receive power and riches and wisdom and might and honor and glory and blessing,' (Revelation 5:12). Think for a moment of the time you felt the closest to God, experiencing the fullest measure of His love for you. Heaven, for your loved one, at this very moment, is infinitely greater than that.

Secondly, your loved one is not only in the presence of thousands of angels and the four living creatures, but he is also with all the saints of all the ages and with Jesus Christ Himself. He is now with Abraham, Isaac, Jacob, Joseph, Moses, David, Paul and Peter and the other apostles. Think of the great heroes of the faith, men like Martin Luther, John Calvin, Jonathan Edwards, George Whitefield, Martyn Lloyd-Jones and lesser saints whom few know but who were nonetheless mighty in Spirit. Your loved one is with them, giving unfettered praise and adoration to the King of Kings and Lord of Lords. And as wonderful and glorious as this is, the greatest of all truths is that he is now looking into the face of the glorified Christ who gave His life for him. He now sees Jesus in His glorified state, and we are told in Revelation 1 that Jesus in His glorified state has eyes as a flame of fire, His feet are like burnished bronze made to glow in a furnace, His face is shining like the sun in all its strength, His head and hair are white like wool, like snow, and His voice is like the sound of many waters. In His right hand are seven stars and out of His mouth comes a sharp two-edged sword.

We have a somewhat different description of His glorified state in Revelation 19. There we are told that as heaven was opened John saw Jesus sitting on a white horse, clothed in white garments, a golden crown is on His head. He is called by the saints and angels in heaven 'Faithful and True.' In righteousness He judges and wages war. He has a sharp two-edged sword coming out of His mouth and with it He smites the nations and rules them with a rod of iron. He wears a robe dipped in blood, and His name is called the "Word of God", and He treads the wine press of the fierce wrath of God the Almighty. On His robe and on His thigh He has a name written, 'King of Kings and Lord of Lords.' What an awesome sight!

My friend, our eyes have not seen, nor have our ears heard, nor has it entered our thoughts, all that God has prepared for those who love Him (1 Corinthians 2:9). Think for a moment of the most glorious thought you can garner. It pales in comparison with the glory that awaits all blood bought sinners who have run to Jesus for refuge. This is the condition of your loved one who has left this life and entered into the presence of Jesus Christ in His glory.

Thirdly, your loved one has now entered into a perfect rest from all his labors. He has entered the New Zion, the new Jerusalem of God, the city of the heavenly king. Hebrews speaks of Zion as being our rest. I have known people who were sexually abused as children and who, though becoming Christians later in life, have still battled the emotional scars of their past. They seem to sabotage their marriages. They tend to be highly manipulative with their adult children. Their children really cannot trust them with their own children because of emotional instability. This, of course, is so very painful for them.

And perhaps you know something of the pain your loved one suffered when his wife left him for another man many years ago. The rejection he experienced never seemed to leave him. He withdrew more and more into a shell. Or maybe he suffered from some sort of bi-polar disorder. There were times when he was very lucid and hungry for the things of God. But there were other times when the 'demons' of his past seemed to conquer him and he was given to outbursts of anger and vile speech. Or maybe toward the end, when the pain medication was making him act in very strange ways, he was given to blasphemy and lewd comments about women he possibly knew and had been with many years before he became a Christian. These are the hard times battered saints often experience near the end of their lives, and you have witnessed many of them.

Or maybe your loved one faced incredible opposition in his professional life. He experienced much loss of business, friendship, and influence over the years. He had many wins but he also had many losses. This put great stress on his marriage. You heard the whispers about his business dealings and you often wondered if they were true or not. You remember the time he lost everything in a fire which destroyed his place of business and he went into deep depression for several years and was simply not himself.

You also remember the strong stand he took for Christ in the workplace which often cost him friends and business. He was valiant for truth and was misunderstood by many as he served as a watchman on the wall, warning the church of heresy and coming judgment while people dismissed him as an alarmist. He left two churches because of heresy and this caused many of his friends to view him as divisive and he no doubt did have an edge to him at times.

But now, my friend, this is all over for him. He has entered his eternal rest. He has entered into the presence of the Lord Jesus who loved him and gave Himself for him. He is perfectly at peace and rest. No more struggle, no more fighting, no more erratic behavior.

And fourthly, your loved one is now endowed with absolute moral perfection. You know that he had faith in Jesus Christ. You know also that he had 'skeletons in his closet.' There were certain sins that he continued to battle. On the one hand, you were convinced of his faith in Jesus Christ and you saw evidence of his hunger for the word of God, prayer, and fellowship with believers. However, on the other hand he battled anger, jealously, and bitterness. He went in and out of porn addiction. He fell into alcohol abuse and drunkenness more than once. You sometimes wondered if he had saving faith, but he always seemed humble and contrite after a period of time. You knew his sins. Everyone in the family knew his sins. You heard people at his funeral speaking in glowing terms of his Christian character and yes, that was true to some extent; but it was also true that he was woefully flawed in many other areas. But at the moment of his death, when his soul was separated from his body, his soul was made absolutely perfect. There was no longer any indwelling sin. He no longer battled the flesh, the old way of living which, from time to time, gained control of him. Nor was he any longer tempted by the world or the devil.

The writer to the Hebrews speaks of the spirits of the righteous made perfect, (Hebrews 12:23). Your loved one was righteous in that he had received the imputed righteousness of Jesus Christ, what we call justification, at his conversion when he repented and believed the gospel. But his daily life of sanctification was more like three steps forward and two steps backward, or sometimes it seemed his sanctification was two steps forward and three steps backward. At death, however, his justified spirit was made perfect. His indwelling sin, flesh, mind, and will were utterly and completely transformed into perfection.

Therefore, my friend, as you grieve the loss of your loved one, please understand that you grieve but not as those who have no hope (1 Thessalonians 4:13). And why should you not grieve as the world grieves? Well, consider these three comforting truths. First, at the death of your loved one, our Lord Jesus received a partial fulfillment of His eternal purpose. In Ephesians 1:4 we read that God chose us in Christ before the foundation of the world, that we should be holy and blameless before Him. So why did God choose us to be His children? In order that we should be holy (having no sin) and blameless (having no guilt). Paul puts it a little differently in Colossians 1 when he says that though we were formerly alienated, hostile in mind, and engaged in evil, God has now reconciled us to Himself through Christ's death to make us holy (without sin), blameless (without guilt) and beyond reproach (without shame). In other words, Christ's desire for all of His blood bought saints is to present us holy and blameless before His

Father. The graduation of your loved one to glory is another stone added to the temple in the New Jerusalem.

We can also say that Jesus gains His great desire. In His high priestly prayer of John 17, Jesus prays, 'Father, I desire that those whom Thou gavest to Me shall be with Me where I am, that they may see My glory. For Thou hast loved Me before the foundation of the world,' (John 17:24). In other words, Jesus desires earnestly for all of His people to spend eternity with Him in heaven. So, when your loved was diagnosed with the inoperable brain tumor you began to pray for his healing. You asked the elders of the church to anoint him with oil and pray for his healing. Prayer went throughout the entire church for his healing. You also made sure he received the best medical care available. But it became clear in the last several months of his life, that Jesus was preparing to bring him to Himself. Jesus' desire was for your loved one to be with Him very soon. You were praying one way, and Jesus was praying to His Father in the opposite way. But at your loved one's death, Jesus received the fulfillment of His desire. So comfort yourself, my friends, with the knowledge that Jesus has gained a partial fulfillment of His great desire and purpose. He wanted your loved one with Him. Do you believe this, my friend? Are you trusting Jesus in this situation?

But we can also go further. Secondly, realize what your Christian loved one has gained. He now has perfect peace, perfect rest, and perfect worship. You know he lived with turmoil most of his days. He was in a highly competitive work environment and he often came home with great emotional stress. He made some difficult and unpopular stands on ethical issues in his company and faced significant pushback. He was maligned by many, and falsely accused by others. But at his death he entered perfect peace, rising far above the fray of all that he faced while on earth.

He also gained perfect rest from the many demands placed on him. He seemed always to attract people with problems and spent countless hours attempting to help them through them. Because he had a great deal of money entrepreneurs were always pitching their latest project to him. Ministries were constantly asking him to invest in what they were doing for the Lord. And his children and grandchildren were constantly asking him to help with their college or post-graduate degree programs. These demands and requirements seemed endless at times, but he continued on, considering their every request. But he is finished with all that now. He is at perfect rest with the Father and the Holy Spirit through the finished work of the Lord Jesus Christ.

And he also has gained perfect rest from all of his labors. There were times in which God gave him His peace which passes all understanding. He knew that when he passed through the fire he would never be scorched, nor would the flame burn him. When he passed through the waters, they would never overflow him or drown him. Why? Because God was his Savior, the Holy One of Israel. But your loved one battled his cancer for over two years. He went through all the prescribed remedies to arrest or slow down the continued spreading of the dreaded disease. He was tired physically, emotionally, and spiritually, You were tired too. His illness affected your entire family. All of you had no choice but to change your plans for trips and business operations. But now he has rest, and though you miss him terribly, you also are at rest.

I have seen families, the night or day after the death of one who had been ill for an extended time period, being joyful, laughing, and having a great time. At first this seems odd, but a sense of relief has come because the Christian loved one is at rest with Jesus in heaven.

And now your loved one in heaven is enjoying perfect, unhindered, uninterrupted worship in heaven. Again, with all the angels, elders, living creatures, and saints, he is now singing a new song, 'Holy, holy, holy is the Lord . . . Worthy is the Lamb that was slain to receive power and riches and wisdom and might and honor, and glory, and blessing.' While the living creatures are giving glory, majesty, dominion and authority, twenty-four elders are constantly falling down to worship the King.

Let's imagine that you could talk with your loved one who is now in heaven, which, of course, there is no indication in Scripture that this is possible. Nonetheless, if possible you might say, 'I worshipped God this morning but my mind wandered. I simply had a difficult time focusing on reading the Bible and praying. I even fell asleep at one point. I attended morning and evening worship today and the sermons were very helpful but even there I found my mind wandering. I guess I convinced myself that I already knew all of this and I was a little bored with the sermon.'

To this your loved one in heaven would no doubt respond, 'I have been praying and worshipping God all day. In fact I have been worshipping Him all day, everyday ever since I got here. I am never bored because our loving Savior is constantly revealing new things to me. I never get sleepy here in heaven, for there is no need for sleep. I am experiencing a constant unfolding of the immensity of our Savior's glorious attributes. I am never weary of praising our great King.'

And thirdly, dear saints, remember what both you and your loved one have gained by his death and translation to heaven. You both have the hope of a glorified body. Paul takes up this glorious issue in great detail in 1 Corinthians 15. Because Jesus was raised from the dead He is the first fruits of those who sleep. We all will also be raised from the dead, and though our bodies are sown perishable bodies, they will be raised imperishable bodies. Though they are sown in dishonor, they will be raised in glory. Though they are sown in weakness they will be raised in power. Though they are sown natural bodies they will be raised spiritual bodies (I Corinthians 15:42-44). Paul also tells us that we are waiting for our adoption as sons, the redemption of our body (Romans 8:23-25). He says our citizenship is in heaven, from which we eagerly wait for a Savior, the Lord Jesus Christ, who will transform the body of our humble estate into conformity with the glory of His body by the exertion of His power to make all things in subjection to Him (Philippians 3:20).

I want to encourage you to live with great hope. Your loved one will receive a glorified body. Paul the apostle, in 1 Corinthians 15, gloriously finishes out his

message of the benefits of Christ's resurrection, 'Behold I tell you a mystery, we shall not all sleep but we shall all be changed in a moment, in the twinkling of an eye, at the last trumpet; for the trumpet shall sound, and the dead will be raised imperishable, and we shall be changed. For this perishable must put on the imperishable, and the mortal must put on immortality. But when this perishable will have put on the imperishable, and this mortal will have put on immortality, then will come about the saying that is written, Death is swallowed up on victory. O death, where is your victory? O death, where is your sting? The sting of death is sin, and the power of sin is the law; but thanks be to God, who gives us the victory through our Lord Jesus Christ. Therefore, my beloved brethren, be steadfast, immovable, always abounding in the work of the Lord, knowing that your toil in the Lord is not in vain in the Lord,'
(1 Corinthians 15:50-58).

I remember speaking with a man I knew who was dying with AIDS. He was a homosexual who had contracted the disease through his many years of sexual liaisons with other men. I asked him, "How do you feel?" He wept and said that he was afraid to die. From there I told him of the glory of heaven which awaits every true believer, going over most of what I have just communicated to you. I told him this could be his if he would repent and truly believe that Jesus died for Him. He called on the name of the Lord to save him, and six days later he was gone. I expect to see him in heaven one day. This is the hope of every true Christian.

This is the hope for you, as well, if you are trusting Jesus Christ alone to save you. Are you truly *believing? Come to Jesus right this very moment. Do not wait. You have no guarantee of living another day. Today is the day of salvation for you. Forsake all and trust Him now.*

Hell: What's It Like, Who Goes There, When, and Why?

These will go away into eternal punishment, but the righteous into eternal life, Matthew 25:46.

I have read where 1.8 people die every second in the world. That's 108 every minute, 6480 every hour, 155,520 every day, 56,764,800 every year. And while we, of course, do not know the exact number of those who descend into hell, surely the number is vast.

We saw last night what exactly happens to the believer in Jesus Christ at his death, that his soul appears immediately in heaven before the Lord Jesus, that he is delivered into perfect peace, rest, and holiness, being filled with inexpressible joy. But now let's ask the question, what is hell like and who goes there? This, my dear friends, is a very sobering message. To ask the question another way, when the non-Christian dies, what happens to him that very moment?

The text I just read is the very end of the so called Olivet Discourse given by Jesus just prior to His arrest, trial, crucifixion, death, and resurrection (Matthew 23-25). He prophesies that the temple would soon be destroyed through a judgment from His Father. Jesus had just wept over Jerusalem because they were unwilling to come to Him and find peace. He knew that a righteous judgment would soon fall. He speaks of perilous times which were soon to come upon Jerusalem and the Jewish people. He speaks next of His glorious return when

He will gather His elect from the four winds, from one end of the sky to another. Jesus then gives a series of parables (of the fig tree, of the ten virgins, of the talents, and of the sheep and goats) which are meant to awaken the Jews to their impending doom if they remain unrepentant. Until the very end Jesus was seeking to win the Jews to Himself. His parables were meant to cut their hearts and move them to bow before Him as their Messiah. In the parable of the sheep and goats He says, "Come, you who are blessed of My Father, inherit the kingdom prepared for you from the foundation of the world. For I was hungry, and you gave Me something to eat; I was thirsty, and you gave Me drink; I was a stranger, and you invited Me in; naked, and you clothed Me; I was a sick, and you visited Me; I was in prison, and you came to Me." When they asked when they did this, Jesus replied, "To the extent that you did it to one of these brothers of Mine, even the least of them, you did it to Me." Jesus is speaking here of showing kindness to those who are following Him. He concludes His parable of the sheep and the goats by saying, "Depart from Me, accursed ones, into the eternal fire which has been prepared for the devil and his angels; for I was hungry, and you gave Me nothing to eat; I was thirsty, and you gave Me nothing to drink; I was a stranger, and you did not invite Me in; naked, and you did not clothe Me; sick, and in prison, and you did not visit Me." "When," they ask, in horror and astonishment, "did we see You in such a destitute state?" Jesus replied that to the extent they did not do this to one of the least of these, they did not do it to Him. Those who obeyed Jesus were the sheep who would enter into eternal life, but the goats were those who had rejected Him. They went away into eternal punishment.

My dear friends, without question, without equivocation, there is a heaven to be gained and a hell to be rejected. Last night our focus was on the wonderful hope of eternal life for the Christian. It is glorious and comforting. But our task tonight is to stress what happens to the unbeliever at death. He will go away into eternal punishment. What does that mean? Jesus is referring to hell. What is hell like, who goes there, when, and why?

Let's address each of these questions. What is hell like? Hell is the intermediate state of every unbeliever at death. I remind you that the intermediate state is a theological term used to denote the place or condition of every person who dies. This does not refer to the final state for that is either the new heaven and new earth or the lake of fire. Jesus spoke far more of hell than any of the apostles or prophets. In fact we can clearly say that Jesus is the one who develops and fully expounds the doctrine of hell. In Matthew 5:29,30 Jesus speaks of those men who look on women in a lustful manner, calling them adulterers. He says that if their right hand causes them to stumble or if their eye causes them to stumble then they are to cut off their hand, they are to pluck out their eye lest they be cast into hell.

In Mark 9:43,44 Jesus is giving a dire warning to men who are stumbling blocks to children. Jesus has just taken a little child into His arms and blessed him. Then He says that whoever causes one of these little ones who have believed in Him to stumble or fall into sin by their own ungodly examples, will go into hell, the unquenchable fire. Jesus doubles down in the next verse and says they will be cast into hell. Later in the same passage Jesus says, while citing Isaiah 66:24, that they will be cast into hell where their worm never dies and the fire is never quenched. What does this mean? Worms die daily. They have very short lives. But here Jesus is saying that hell is eternal, a place where the lowly worm never dies. Jesus can also be alluding to the lowly state of the damned sinner who is away forever from the presence of the Lord and His glory. When he says the fire is never quenched He means hell fire will never end. It is eternal. This also means that those recipients of hell fire will never be destroyed. Fire, if hot enough, melts and destroys everything. This fire, however, will never destroy the souls in hell. Hell is endless, conscious torment.

Jesus also refers to hell as the place of death, or Hades. In the parable of the so called rich man and Lazarus (Luke 16:19-31), Jesus says the rich man is in hell and he lifts up his eyes in a state of torment. He asks God to show him mercy through Father Abraham, but there is no mercy there. He begs for some measure of relief from his thirst by having Lazarus come from heaven to dip the tip of his finger in water and cool off his tongue, but none is coming. He speaks of being "in agony in these flames." How bad must it be for a man to beg with all his might for a drop of water hopefully to satisfy his dreadful thirst. He also begs the Father to send Lazarus to his loved ones and warn them of their impending judgment. But there is no hope in hell. It is a place of conscience, endless, unquenchable fire, and unmitigated, just suffering and torment.

To go further, in the parable of the slighted marriage feast, when all the guests are celebrating the feast with the King's son and his new wife, there is one there without the necessary wedding clothes. When confronted by the king, the man was speechless, a picture of all who stand before the judgment seat of Christ and give account of all their deeds done in the body, whether good or bad. Jesus tells us in the parable that the man without the wedding clothes is bound hand and foot and cast into outer darkness where there is weeping and gnashing of teeth (Matthew 22:1-14).

This description of outer darkness and weeping and the gnashing of teeth is a very vivid picture of the horror and hopelessness all condemned sinners experience in hell, the place of unimaginable horror and suffering. Those in the outer darkness of hell are all alone. They never see another person. Recently I heard of a man who bet that he could stay in a darkened bathroom for thirty days without communication with anyone, without any sunlight. He could not last. He was going crazy. He had no concept of time because he never had the sun to inform him of a new day. The gnashing of teeth reminds me of the horror of those poor Jews in the Nazi concentration camps as the showers with poison gas were poured on them. In pain, horror, and hopelessness many of them bit themselves and other naked bodies dying with them. Those in hell are weeping because they know what they lost. People weep when they lose something dear to them. Those in hell know they have lost their souls and there is absolutely nothing they can do to arrest the situation. There is nothing they can do to deliver themselves from it. They can look back and remember the opportunities they had to call on Christ, and how they rejected the overtures of grace to them. But now it is too late. Now they are lost. Now they are in hell forever.

So, to sum up what Jesus is saying is this—hell is a place of conscious, eternal, torment, in isolation and darkness reserved for all condemned sinners.

We can go further and say that hell is a place of justice. The justice of God, giving people their due based on their actions, thoughts, speech, and values, is grounded on God's holiness. God will by no means leave the guilty unpunished. Paul the Apostle, in summarizing his teaching in Romans on the universality of sin, writes:

"There is none righteous, not even one. There is none who understands, there is none who seeks for God. All have turned aside, together they have become useless. There is none who does good, there is not even one. Their throat is an open grave, with their tongues they keep deceiving, the poison of asps is under their lips, their feet are swift to shed innocent blood, destruction and misery are in their paths, and the path of peace they have not known. There is no fear of God before their eyes," (Romans 3:11-18).

And how does God execute His justice on sinners? Paul says,"For after all it is only just for God to repay with affliction those who afflict you, and to give relief to you who are afflicted and to us as well when the Lord Jesus will be revealed from heaven with His mighty angels in flaming fire, dealing out retribution to those who do not know God and to those who do not obey the gospel of our Lord Jesus. These will pay the penalty of eternal destruction away from the presence of the Lord and from the glory of His power, when He comes to be glorified in His saints on that day, and to be marveled at among all who have believed," (2 Thessalonians 1:6-10).

Paul also says that the kindness of God (all of the nice things God has given us for our own enjoyment) is meant to lead us to repentance. In other words, when we consider all of the earthly and material blessings we have, then we should say to ourselves, "God has been very good to me. I should obey Him. I should submit to Him and live for Him." This, however, does not happen. We tend to attribute our good success to our own abilities and hard work. Consequently Paul says that we are storing up for ourselves wrath in a day of wrath and revelation of the righteous judgment of God who will render to every man according to his deeds.

Think of a fifty-five gallon drum resting under a gutter running from the roof of a house in a tropical rain forest in Brazil. The water runs off during the rain into the barrel. The more rain, the more quickly the barrel fills with water. Finally the barrel overflows. The longer one lives without seeking God in the person and work of Jesus Christ, then the greater are his sins, and the greater is his impending judgment. It is far better for a rebellious sinner to die at the age of eighteen than sixty-five. Why? The longer one lives, the longer he sins, and the greater the number of his sins. Consequently the greater his judgment will be from the Holy One. God's wrath is constantly increasing with the condemned sinner. One day His patience will end and the sinner will be cast into hell.

What are you doing, my friends, with the goodness of God manifested to you in multitudinous ways? What are you going to do with God? Are you hardhearted? Are you unrepentant? Your sins daily, my friend, are mounting up against you. The longer you live, the greater your judgment and coming condemnation. If you are not in Christ, then you are now under the wrath of God and only His mercy is keeping you from hell this very moment.

Do not be deceived, my friends. God is not mocked. He is just. He is holy. He must and He will punish sin. No guilty person will be spared.

Furthermore, hell is certain. No condemned sinner will ever escape the just judgment of God upon ungodly sinners who have lived in ungodly ways, and said ungodly things. We saw this earlier in the Luke 16 passage concerning the rich man and Lazarus. Those in hell know exactly where they are. They are not unconscious. They are not annihilated. They are not in some comatose state. They are in a disembodied state, but they nonetheless are conscious where they are. They are in hell.

In the Song of Moses, just prior to Israel's entrance into the Promise Land, Moses speaks these very sobering words, "Vengeance is Mine, and retribution. In due time their foot will slip; for the day of their calamity is near, and the impending things are hastening upon them," (Deuteronomy 32:35). The unbeliever does not know the day of God's vengeance. It may come today or next week, or fifty years from now, but that day is coming.

But how might that happen? Perhaps you will die suddenly in an automobile on your way to work as you hit a patch of black ice and veer into on-coming traffic. You may die in a plane accident on take off when a small single engine plane mistakenly wanders into your air space and collides with the jet on which you are traveling. Maybe you will be murdered in a late night holdup at a convenience store as you innocently wait in line to pay for your gallon of milk. It may be that you die at work from a massive heart attack. Maybe you will be diagnosed with liver cancer and be told you have three months to live, that you better get your house in order. Perhaps your children will die before you, something that always saddens any parent. Or maybe you will live to a ripe old age and die in your bed with your family around you. But however it happens, in whatever circumstances, at whatever age, you know the truth of what Jesus and the apostles are saying—you will die!

When least expected, your foot will slip from the ledge on the cliff, hurling you to your death below on the rocks of the shore. It is a sure, certain, and terrifying judgment.

But why this certain and just judgment upon sinners? Isn't it true that God is in the forgiveness business? Can't He look the other way at our sin? No, of course not. But why not? I referred to this earlier but I wish to explore it in greater detail now. Paul asks us, "Do you not know that the kindness of God is meant to lead you to repentance?" (Romans 2:5). That is, every unbeliever ought to see the goodness of God in all areas of his life. When he wakes up in the morning in his nice home with heat and central air conditioning, when he takes a hot shower in his nice bathroom, when he drinks a nice cup of coffee and eats a hearty breakfast before work, when he drives his expensive luxury car to his office where he makes a very nice salary, when he must go to a doctor for health care and is given the best care possible, all of these and many more are from the hand of God. Consequently, as Paul is saying, every unbeliever should be drawn to Christ in repentance due to God's manifold blessings on his life. But Paul goes further to say that this is not what happens at all. They are unrepentant. They are unwilling to surrender to Jesus, the Lord. They are unwilling to admit their own rebellion against God. They therefore are stirring up wrath for themselves in the day of the just wrath of God which is being poured out on all unrepentant sinners. To stir up wrath is like the student in Middle School who has been bullied incessantly all year long. He has finally had enough, and he erupts and beats down his opponents in a fit of rage on the playground. You have maligned God. You have "bullied Him" by blaspheming Him and flagrantly disobeying Him. His wrath may soon be kindled, and then, what shall you do?

Your sin is mounting up, my friends, and you face a certain terrifying expectation of judgment. Do you really think you will escape the judgment of God when you have repeatedly trampled under foot the Son of God, have regarded as unclean and ineffectual the blood of Jesus which the Bible repeatedly says saves and sanctifies, and have insulted the Holy Spirit by rejecting His many overtures of grace to you? Deuteronomy 28:15-68 is a graphic, sordid list of judgments which were coming upon Israel if they moved from obeying the true and living God and went after the idols of the nations they were dispossessing. Among other things they were told that the Lord would send curses, confusion, and rebuke until they were quickly destroyed. A man would look on as other men violate his wife. They would be robbed and oppressed repeatedly with no one to save them. They would sow much seed but gather little. The alien would rise higher and higher and they would go down lower and lower. Refined and delicate women would secretly eat their own children due to the lack of food. Pestilence would overtake them. They would be routed by their enemies and the Lord would smite them with madness, blindness, and bewilderment. The list of judgments against Israel serve as a graphic picture of hell for you and any unrepentant sinner anywhere in the world.

Are you ready to meet God, my friend? There is no more important question. In your present, unregenerate state, you will die in your sins.

Finally, we can say that hell is a place of eternal torment. John Stott, near the end of his ministry, espoused the view that when people die and go to hell, their souls eventually will be consumed in hell fire and thus annihilated. Stott's position is very disappointing and clearly unbiblical. I wish that were true for that would lessen the horror of hell to some degree. But there is no indication of this in Scripture. In fact there is just the opposite. Peter speaks of the souls now in prison (1 Peter 3:19). John speaks of unbelievers being cast into the lake of fire and brimstone where the beast and the false prophets are also and they will be tormented day and night forever and ever (Revelation 20:10).

Actually, to be more specific, hell is not eternal though judgment is eternal. Those now in hell would give anything they had if it would only allow them to stay in hell for another million years. Why? Because hell will be destroyed and all the lost, damned, and condemned sinners will be cast into the lake of fire on the day of the Great White Throne judgment (Revelation 20:11-15). I will have much more to say about this on Wednesday night.

The very fact that judgment is eternal tells us all we need to know about the heinous and seditious nature of our sin. Sin is rebellion against the Creator and Sustainer of all life. It is rebellion against the lover of our souls. A teen-aged young man who has lived with loving and caring parents, who nonetheless, turns against them and murders them, will rightly be seen as an ungrateful, manipulative, murderous, and vile person. People will have no trouble believing that he should be punished for his rebellion.

But this raises another vital question. Who goes to hell? The answer, my friends, to this question is that every unbeliever goes to hell upon his death. We have no trouble believing that murderers, rapists, child abusers, kidnappers, and drug dealers deserve hell. Why? Because they tend to destroy others. But moral sinners also go to hell. Your nice neighbor who collects your mail and feeds your pets when you are on your vacation, but who has never closed with Christ, is also under a terrifying, expectation of God's judgment. But even religious people go to hell as well. Hell is no doubt full of Presbyterians, Baptists, Methodists, Charismatics, and Roman Catholics. Hell is also full of Hindus, Buddhists, Muslims, and secularists. Jesus made this fact clear when He said, "I am the Way, the Truth, and the Life. No one comes to the Father but through Me," (John 14:6). Peter said that there is salvation in no one else; for there is no

29

other name under heaven given among men by which we must be saved (Acts 4:12). Hell is also full of people who once made a profession of faith in Jesus Christ. Jesus said, at the end of His Sermon on the Mount, "Not everyone who says, 'Lord, Lord' will enter into heaven; but he who does the will of My Father who is in heaven, he is the one who will enter into heaven," (Matthew 7:21). Mere lip service to the King is not true deliverance and salvation.

Perhaps you have been a church goer all your life, and you well remember calling on the name of the Lord to save you. But as the years have passed, you have drifted away from the faith you once held dear. And can you not see clearly how the material and temporal pursuits in your life now swamp or overrun the spiritual? Making money, putting food on the table, saving for a vacation, all seemed more important at the time than prayer, reading the Bible, teaching your children about God, or bringing them to church every Sunday. You probably did not mean for this to happen, but it occurred nonetheless. You had good intentions, but these have been pushed out of your weekly regimen. You have been drifting away from the Lord.

The moral can also inundate the holy. You very possibly buy into the counterfeit of true Biblical holiness. Holiness means living according to God's word. But perhaps you tend to think that being a good neighbor, helping your child through the *Boy Scout* program, as good as these things are, is the real thing. There is absolutely nothing wrong with the *Boy Scouts* or being a good neighbor. I applaud that, of course. But this is not the same as Biblical holiness, where one seeks to live *Coram Deo*, before the face of God, seeking more than anything His smile on our actions, speech, and values, and dreading more than anything His frown upon them.

So are you drifting away from the vital things of life? Are you allowing the urgent to crowd out the important, the temporal to drown out the eternal, the material to swamp the spiritual, the moral to inundate the holy?

You still, however, hold onto that experience you had many years before. But the question now, my friend, is this. Do you have any evidence that Christ, the hope of glory, resides in you? Paul summarizes his teaching on the universality of sin by saying, "All have sinned and fallen short of the glory of God," (Romans 3:23).

But when does this death leading you to hell come upon you? We don't know how or when. Perhaps you will die tonight on your way home from this meeting. Perhaps you will die next week at your favorite restaurant as you choke on a steak. Maybe you have been very tired for some time and have been losing weight. So you make an appointment with your family doctor who runs several tests and comes back with a diagnosis of pancreatic cancer. He gives you three months to live. Or maybe you live to a ripe old age of ninety-five and die in your bed at home with your children, grand-children, and great grand-children standing around your bed as you breathe your last breath. But you are certain of this one thing, you will die.

So, here's what happens to the unbeliever the moment he dies. His soul immediately leaves his body and goes straight to hell. He is in a place of inexhaustible, indescribable, and unmitigated horror. Those in hell are conscious of where they are and their condition. They are in misery and torment. They are burning but not consumed because, after all, they are only at this juncture disembodied souls. Hell is a fire that is never quenched, never extinguished. Furthermore, hell is a place where the worm never dies. What does this mean? Most commentators suggest this refers to the awful reality that those in hell now realize their failed opportunities to respond to the gospel while they were living on earth. They now remember the faithful Sunday school teacher or the Vacation Bible School leader who told them of Christ, but they refused the offer of grace. They remember their college roommate who told them of Jesus and invited them repeatedly to the *Campus Crusade for Christ* weekly meetings, but they never got around to going to them. They remember the work associate who coaxed them to attend an Easter service where they remember now vividly hearing a clear presentation of the gospel, but they rejected it. Now they know they are receiving exactly what they deserve, hell, separation from the glory of God in a place of utter misery and doom.

But my friends, no one must go to hell. Jesus died for sinners just like you and me.

But how do you remove your guilt? How can you remedy the certain, terrifying expectation of the judgment in hell which is coming upon you? You must call on the name of the Lord Jesus to save you. What does this mean? Paul the Apostle says that God made Jesus, who knew no sin, to become sin on our behalf, that we might become the righteousness of God in Christ (2 Corinthians 5:21). Paul also says that Christ is the propitiation in His blood through faith (Romans 3:25). Propitiation means atoning sacrifice. The Apostle John also uses this term in 1 John 2:2, and 4:10. So Jesus, the perfect, sinless, undefiled Son of God, came into the world and lived in perfect obedience to His father. He presented Himself on the cross at Calvary, to bear our sins in His body, that He might reconcile us to the Father. When Psalm 5 says that God abhors or hates the man of bloodshed and deceit, and we couple this with 2 Corinthians 5:21, then we begin to realize the amazing transaction which took place two thousand years ago just outside Jerusalem. Your sins–your murderous lifestyle, your deceit, idolatry, murder, enmity, strife, deceit, malice, arrogance, pride, fornication, adultery, homosexuality, outbursts of anger, disputings, factions, and envyings–were all placed on Jesus on the cross. Jesus became a propitiation, an atoning sacrifice, for you, taking your sin upon Himself, suffering the hell which you deserve. When Jesus cried out, "My God, My God, why hast Thou forsaken Me?" (Matthew 27:46), He was looking for comfort and mercy from His Father, but His Father was silent. We know that for those three hours on the cross the perfect, holy God actually hated His Son!

My friend, can there be anything more glorious than the death and resurrection of Jesus Christ? Call on him now to save you.

And if you are already a Christian, then marvel, my friends, at what God has wrought in your heart. Thank Him daily for saving your soul. Always be amazed at the grace of God in your life. He has delivered you, by His death, from sin, sickness, Satan, hell, and death. Now let others know of God's great saving work in you.

The New Earth: Can It Really Be Better Than Heaven?

Then I saw a new heaven and a new earth, for the first heaven and the first earth passed away, and there is no longer any sea. And I saw the holy city, the new Jerusalem, coming down out of heaven from God, made ready as a bride adorned for her husband. And I heard a loud voice from the throne saying, "Behold, the tabernacle of God is among men, and He will dwell among them, and they shall be His people, and God Himself will be among them, and He will wipe away every tear from their eyes; and there will no longer be any death; there will no longer be any mourning, or crying or pain; the first things have passed away.

And He who sits on the throne said, "Behold, I am making all things new." And He said, "Write for these words are faithful and true." Then He said to me, "It is done. I am the Alpha and the Omega, the beginning and the end. I will give to the one who thirsts from the spring of the water of life without cost. He who overcomes will inherit these things, and I will be his God and he will be My son." Revelation 21:1-7.

From April 7 to mid July, 1994, the Hutu majority in Rwanda capped off years of hatred between the Hutu and Tutsi tribes by unleashing a horrible genocide where marauding hoards of Hutu hacked and slashed to death with machetes nearly 1 million Tutsis. The killing of Sub-Saharan Christians in Sudan by the Muslim majority, along with the bombing by Russian made bombers and helicopter gunships of black Christians, Muslims, and animists in the Nuba mountains are well documented examples of modern day genocide. In 1984 our fourth son Patrick was born with numerous birth defects and lived six weeks before dying in the Neo-natal unit at Kennestone Hospital in Marietta, Georgia. And may I say that it is altogether possible that someone here tonight has watched a loved one waste away over several years with some terrible disease. Why do these terrible atrocities happen? Why must we watch helplessly as our loved ones die a slow, painful death?

There are only two types of people in the world, and both of you are here tonight. I imagine that the vast majority of you are Christians. You have been born again by the work of the Holy Spirit. You give evidence of faith in Christ. He has and is transforming your life. The Holy Spirit has born witness with your spirit that you are children of God. However, there very possibly could be some here tonight who, though very nice people, are perhaps even faithful church goers for many years, but who are still not Christians. You have the form of godliness but there is no substance.

Let's imagine, for a moment, that you receive a death sentence from your physician. You have an aggressive form of pancreatic cancer and you are told that you have six months to live. How may I encourage you? What can I say to you who are not Christians? Unbeliever, what can I say to drive you to jealousy? After all, the world is filled with sorrow, injustice, disease, and death. Where is God in the face of these horrible atrocities and tragedies we face from time to time? Is there any word from God to make sense of the mess in which we find ourselves in this world? Yes there is. Consider the text I just read to you.

The Apostle John, while in prison for his faith on the Isle of Patmos, receives a series of visions and revelations from the resurrected and glorified Savior and Lord, Jesus Christ. The churches of Asia Minor, to whom Jesus writes His seven letters (Revelation 2,3), are urged to persevere in the faith, regardless of the hardships and persecutions under which they were currently living. These dear believers were being severely persecuted by the agents of the Roman Empire. They also were getting it from the Jewish leaders. They were sorely tempted to walk away from the faith. It is within this context that John receives his revelation from Jesus Christ. The conflict with the harlot, the beast, and the false prophet were overcome by the resurrected and glorified Christ. The book of Revelation was written to encourage God's people of Asia Minor who were wondering at times if God really loved them, if they were true recipients of His grace.

So, what is Jesus telling us in the text before us tonight? First, John tells us what he saw. He said, "I saw a new heaven and a new earth." This is not the first time this language has been used in the Bible. Isaiah speaks of the new heaven and the new earth. "For just as the new heavens and the new earth which I make will endure before Me, declares the Lord, so your offspring and your name will endure. And it shall be from the new moon to the new moon and from Sabbath to Sabbath, all mankind will come to bow down before Me, says the Lord. They will go forth and look on the corpses of the men who have transgressed against Me. For their worm will not die and their fire will not be quenched; and they will an abhorrence to all mankind," (Isaiah 66:24).

Isaiah, in preaching to call Israel and Judah back to their covenant with God, paints a picture of contrasts. He reminds us that there will in fact, with all certainty, be a new heaven and a new earth. There will be the restoration of all things. This world as we know it, marred by sin, sickness, death, earthquakes, hurricanes, tornadoes, tsunamis, floods, and fires will end one day. Peter says that it will be burned with fire (2 Peter 3:10). But he also speaks of a new heaven and a new earth, proclaiming with certainty that things will not always continue as they are. There will be a new day, a glorious day, in which all will be changed. He says this in order to drive home to His people the certainty that their offspring will also endure forever. There will be a continual reverence, honor, and commitment to the King of Glory. When speaking of how they will look on the corpses of those who are His enemies, those who have transgressed His law, God is pronouncing a certain judgment on violators of His law. Their destination is hell, the place where the worm will not die and the fire is never quenched.

The Apostle Peter also mentions the new heavens and the new earth. In speaking of the day of the Lord, the day in which God will judge all the people of the world, he says, "But the day of the Lord will come like a thief, in which the heavens will pass away with a roar and the elements will be destroyed with intense heat, and the earth and its works will be burned up. Since all these things are to be destroyed in this way, what sort of people ought you to be in holy conduct and godliness, looking for and hastening the coming of the day of God, because of which the heavens will be destroyed by burning and the elements will melt with intense heat! But according to His promise we are looking for new heavens and a new earth, in which righteousness dwells," (2 Peter 3:10-13).

Note that the present world will be destroyed by the intense heat of fire and the heavens (that is the stars and galaxies) will pass away with a roar. But afterwards God will renew all things by creating new heavens and a new earth. We are commanded by Peter, therefore, to conduct ourselves with godliness, looking for and even hastening or hurrying up the coming day of the Lord, by discipling the nations. Earlier in this passage Peter quotes those who mock such a notion, wondering, "Where is the promise of His coming?" But Peter says that to the Lord a thousand years is as one day and one day is as a thousand years. In other words, our concept of time is limited. We are finite, but God is infinite. He will accomplish His purpose of restoration in His time. It will come like a thief in the night, when it is least expected, when most are at ease, sleeping comfortably, as it were, in their beds when the tumult comes upon them. Therefore every true believer is to walk circumspectly, as Paul puts it (Ephesians 5:15), like a soldier in Iraq clearing a building of the enemy. He walks carefully, weapon drawn, eyes wide open, looking for trouble.

So, why is this restoration of all things created so necessary? After the fall into sin in Genesis 3:1-7, God pronounces judgment on the serpent, woman, and man. The serpent would wage war against the Son of God, seeking to destroy Him. We are told, however, that while the serpent would bruise His heel (orchestrate His crucifixion) the Son would crush his head (utterly destroy him in the lake of fire). Due to her part in the fall into sin, women will suffer the pains of childbirth and their zeal will be for their husbands (a woman's tendency is to dominate her husband, to usurp his responsibility of leadership). And because of the man's disobedience to God he would earn his living by the sweat of his brow and the earth would be filled with thorns and thistles, a picture of how the world naturally disintegrates when left to itself, that life would be filled with hardship and sorrow. He would also naturally neglect his responsibility to lead his wife and children. From that day forward until Christ's second coming, enmity or animosity exists between the devil and Jesus, the Christ. Enmity and strife also exists between husbands and wives. Enmity and hostility exists between one nation and another. We know the Lord Jesus has now conquered sin, death, and Satan, but we still are living in a fallen world where the devil continues to tempt and lead Christ's bondservants away from God.

God's sentence on the woman was to multiply her pain in bringing children into the world and to dominate her husband, to usurp his rightful place as head of he house. Women are prone, ever since, to control the family while the man's tendency is to let her do it. And then there is God's judgment on the man. The ground would be cursed because of disobedience and rebellion. It would yield thorns and thistles, making the work of farming difficult and less productive. And man would earn his living from the sweat of his brow. In other words, work would be tiresome, frustrating, stressful.

And the fall into sin and the consequent imputation of Adam's sin upon all mankind has wrought untold devastation on the world. The world and all of creation was made perfect by God. There was no death, no sickness. Adam and Eve ate the fruit of the trees and food from the garden. But the fall brought the cycle of death and rebirth to creation. Plants and animals die. People die. Moreover people murder other people and foist terrible injustices upon the world. We now have racial bigotry, oppression of various ethnicities around the world. In every country where I have traveled and preached, I witness certain ethnic or tribal groups who are oppressed by others. Racial bigotry is everywhere. Nations war against nations. Families war against families. Marriages break up. Children rebel against their parents. Parents neglect or coddle their children and thus severely weaken them. Storms, hurricanes, tsunamis, tornadoes, earthquakes, floods, and fires all bring great devastation on the world. The world is a mess, but it was not always this way.

This is why the words of Isaiah, Peter, and John are so comforting and encouraging to God's people. God promises to restore all things to their original pristine glory. Think again of what existed prior to Adam and Eve's fall into sin—utter and complete perfection in everything. In proclaiming the promise of a new creation, a new heavens and a new earth, God is promising to right all the wrongs which have ever been done.

Think again of my introductory remarks. Will the injustices in Sudan, Rwanda, and so many other places be rectified? What good has come from God's presence in these places of hardship?

Maybe you were abused by your father or brothers when you were a child. You say that you have forgiven them, released them from their sins against you, but have you? Perhaps you were victimized by a break-in at your home, and you now sleep very erratically. Maybe you were falsely accused and lost your job, and the false accuser seems to have not suffered at all for his lie. Do you have any recourse?

The promise, my dear friend, of a new heaven and a new earth changes everything. So specifically, when will the new heavens and the new earth take place?

"Then I saw an angel coming down from heaven, holding he key of the abyss and a great chain in his hand. And he laid hold of the dragon, the serpent of old, who is the devil and Satan, and bound him for a thousand years; and threw him into the abyss and sealed it over him until the thousand are completed. After this he must be released for a short time," (Revelation 20:1-4).

There are many ways to interpret the binding of the devil, the serpent of old. For several reasons, I believe the view which makes the most sense is that the devil was bound at the beginning of Christ's ministry. Jesus announced His ministry, saying that the kingdom of God had come. The demons on numerous occasions acknowledged Him as having authority over them. And in Matthew 12:29 Jesus speaks of binding the strong man and thus plundering his house. Until Christ's coming the whole world lay in the power of the devil (1John 5:19). The devil had deceived the nations. The nations rise up against the Lord. They devise vain things (Psalm

2:1-3). "They mock and wickedly speak from on high. They have set their mouths against the heavens, and their tongue parades throughout the whole earth," (Psalm 73:8,9). The devil has also blinded the minds of the unbelieving so that they may not see the light of the gospel of the glory of Christ who is the image of God (2 Corinthians 4:6). But Jesus read from Isaiah 61 at the beginning of His ministry, saying that the Spirit of the Lord was upon Him because God anointed Him to preach the gospel to the poor, to proclaim release to the captives, the recovery of sight for the blind, to set free those who are downtrodden, and to proclaim the favorable year of the Lord (Luke 4:18,19). In other words, Jesus was announcing that a "new sheriff" was in town, and He was going to begin the process of renewing that which had been corrupted through enslavement to sin, Satan, and death.

The binding of the devil by the Lord Jesus, which began at Christ's earthly ministry, continues for a "thousand years." I believe this thousand years is a figurative and not literal term. It refers to the entire time period between Jesus' first and second advents. So far, the thousand year reign of Christ has continued for over two thousand years. It will end when Christ comes on the clouds in His glory to establish the new heavens and the new earth.

And what happens to the believer and unbeliever at Christ's second coming? I will address the unbeliever's situation tomorrow night, but what about the believer? Those who are alive on earth at the time of Christ's second coming will be caught up together in the clouds and meet Christ on His return to establish the new heavens and new earth. We read of this in 1 Thessalonians 4:16, "For the Lord Himself will descend from heaven with a shout, with the voice of the archangel, and with the trumpet of God; and the dead in Christ shall rise first. Then, we who are alive and remain shall be caught up together with them in the clouds to meet the Lord in the air, and thus we shall always be with the Lord. Therefore comfort one another with these words." Those who died in Christ, whose souls have been in heaven ever since they died on earth, and have experienced joy inexpressible and full of glory, will then be released from heaven and meet the saints still alive as they are lifted up to meet Jesus. The glorified saints will return with Jesus to the new earth.

However, according to 1 Corinthians 15:42-24, 50-58, due to Christ's resurrection, who is the first fruits of those who are asleep, every believer is promised a glorified body. Paul says that our bodies are sown a perishable body, but they are raised an imperishable body (they will never disintegrate or die). They are sown in dishonor (with sin, sickness, and death), but they are raised in glory. They are sown in weakness (indwelling sin, growing weaker and weaker with every passing year, but also physical, mental, and emotional weaknesses and infirmities) but they are raised in power. They are sown natural bodies (with flesh, bone, ligaments, and blood) and they are raised spiritual bodies. They will bear a resemblance to our earthly bodies but they will also be markedly different. Jesus, in His resurrected state, when first appearing to the woman and disciples, was unidentifiable to them. We will look something like Jesus though we, of course, will not possess His deity or glory.

We also are told in Revelation 21:1-4 that at His second coming the Lord Jesus will make everything new. He will wipe away every tear from our eyes. There will no longer be any death. There will be no more mourning, or crying, or pain. In other words, Jesus will make everything right. He will bring forth justice to the nations. Evil doers will be judged and punished. And throughout eternity the sum total of His glorious attributes will be on full display as He unveils the full manifestation of His sovereign plan for all the ages. At that time you will fully understand why certain bewildering and painful events happened in your life, why you lost a child in infancy, why your suffered the affects of a physical birth defect, why your spouse died a slow, painful death, what good came from the genocide of the Jews, the Tutsis, the Cambodians, and the Sudanese Christians. It will all be revealed to you as you are living in the midst of unimaginable glory, peace, contentment, and joy.

In May, 2001, while pastoring the Golden Isles Presbyterian Church at St. Simons Island, Georgia, I received a phone call from a woman in our community who told me that *Aid Atlanta,* a homosexual advocacy group, was coming to nearby Jekyll Island for a weekend conference called "The Gay Men's Health Summit."

This conference, I was told, would champion homosexuality and the participants would largely be homosexuals themselves. My caller asked what I thought we should do about it, and before I could answer she suggested, "We need to pressure the Jekyll Island Authority to not allow this conference. We ought to boycott the hotel where the conference is to take place. And we ought to buy billboards all over town, voicing our disapproval of the homosexual lifestyle." My response was, "If that is what you are planning, then count me out. I want nothing to do with it." I went on to say, "Now I am willing to train a few men in how to share the gospel of Christ with the men there and to go to the meeting in hopes of showing these people the love of Christ." She said, "Okay, I like your idea better. I will make sure we have twenty-four hour prayer support for your ministry."

So a couple of weeks before the September 11 attack on our country, in late August, 2001, on the Monday afternoon before the conference began, I received a phone call from the manager of the hotel, who by the way, was a member of our church. He told me that *Aid Atlanta* knew I was planning to attend the conference and that if I showed up, they would have me arrested for trespassing. I thought about that for a while and then decided to register for the conference. After all, if I was a paying registrant then I would not be trespassing. I also reserved a room at the hotel so that I could be there with the men. And then I started to think about that scenario — evangelical pastor, at a gay men's conference, by myself, in a hotel room. Doesn't look good. So I asked Wini, my wife, to meet me there at the hotel on Friday night.

Early on my plan was to introduce myself to a few men upon arrival and quickly move into gospel conversations with them. However, along about the Wednesday or Thursday leading up to the conference, I began to sense that that would not be the best approach. So I arrived with two young men from our church and I paid the $200 registration fee and received my purple bag with all sorts of interesting things in it, and my name tag, "Al Baker, Gay Men's Health Summit." I told the people at registration (by the way they knew who I was before I even introduced myself) that our church wished to have a ministry to HIV positive men and we did not have the slightest idea how to do this, that we were there to learn. All the men there, with the exception of one, who I believe was seeking to shock me with his blatant, over- the-top homosexual ambiance, were very gracious and kind to us. I went to numerous seminars on various health issues and, by the way, had several very in depth gospel conversations with practicing homosexuals.

Now the plan was for my wife to meet me at the hotel at 6 p.m. I was waiting for her, standing with two of my new, homosexual acquaintances, when she came into the lobby. When she saw me, she was aghast. I was standing under a sign which read, "Welcome, Gay Men's Health Summit," with a name tag around my neck, "Al Baker, Gay Men's Health Summit," with the purple bag in my hand. I introduced her to my acquaintances, and as we made our way into the restaurant, she said under her breath, "Take off that badge, and put down that bag! Look at you. I am so embarrassed." By the way, Wini has granted me permission to tell this story. So, I put down my bag, took off my badge, and we walked into the restaurant. As we walked to our table we passed table after table of homosexual men and they graciously welcomed her. By the time we got to our table, tears were streaming down her cheeks. She said, "Please forgive me. I am so ashamed of myself. I am a Pharisee. I know my response is sinful." Of course I forgave her and we went on from there to have an amazing ministry with HIV positive, homosexual men, meeting weekly with the them.

One of the first men who attended weekly was forty-three years old at the time, and had been a very well known hair stylist in New York City. By the time I met him he had AIDS and was near the end of his life. I picked him up every Wednesday night for our meeting, which was attended by as many as twenty HIV positive, homosexual men, most of whom by the way, were very poor. I was visiting the former hair stylist one day in his hospice room, and I asked, "How do you feel?" He began to weep, and said, "I am afraid to die." I said, "I understand your fear, but may I tell you what happens to the Christian when he dies?" I went on for about fifteen minutes telling him much of what I told you about heaven on Sunday night. I spoke to him of the glories of heaven, that eye has not seen, ear has not heard, nor has it entered the heart of man all that God has prepared for those who love Him. I then said, "As wonderful as that is, heaven is not the end. It gets even better than that. Your body is wasting away with this dreaded disease, but there is hope for you to receive a glorified body, like what the Lord Jesus has now in heaven." From there I went on to quote to him large sections of 1 Corinthians 15 like, "Behold I tell you a mystery. We shall not all sleep, but we shall be changed, in a moment, in the twinkling of an eye, at the last trumpet. For the trumpet will sound, and the dead shall be raised imperishable, and we shall be changed. For the perishable must put on the ✳ perishable, and the mortal must put on immortality. But when the perishable will have put on the imperishable, and this mortal will have put on immortality, then will come about the saying that is written, 'Death is swallowed up in victory. O death, where is your victory? O death where is your sting?' The sting of death is sin, and the power of sin is the law, but thanks be to God who gives us the victory through our Lord Jesus Christ. Therefore, my beloved brethren be steadfast, immovable, always abounding in the work of the Lord, knowing that your toil in the Lord is not in vain."

I then asked him, "Do you know what this means?" I said, "It means that though you have a body wasting away with this dreaded disease, there is still hope for you. If you call on Christ to save you, then at your death your soul will be with Jesus in perfect peace. As wonderful as that truth is, it gets even better. You will receive a perfect, glorified body. No more disease. No more death. No more sorrow and pain. You will live with Christ forever in His presence, on the new earth. You need not die without Jesus, the great lover of your soul." Then I said, "That's the kind of God I serve. He is ready, quick, and powerful to save, cleanse, and forgive you. Jesus can save you this very minute. There is no need for you to die in your sins and go to hell. Repent, surrender now to Jesus. Say to Him, 'God, be merciful to me a sinner,' and He will forgive you and make you His child." Six days later he was dead, and I have strong reason to believe that God saved him in the last days of his life. I expect to see him in heaven.

What about you, my friends? Are you ready to meet God? Are you confident that when you close your eyes in death you will go immediately to Jesus in heaven? Are you confident that you have honored the King by joyful obedience, and are waiting anxiously for the consummation of the ages in the full and eternal salvation of your soul and glorified body, living with Christ and his holy angels for all eternity?

He is saying to you that He can take your sins from you as far as the east is from the west, that as a father has compassion on his children, so the Lord can show compassion to you, that as far as the heavens are above the earth, so great is His lovingkindness toward those who fear Him. He says that all who believe in His Son have eternal life, and will never perish, and that eternal life begins the moment you believe on Him. He says that all your guilt and shame, all the things you should have done but did not do, all the harmful and hurtful things you said and did to your spouse or children, can and will be forgiven you by the precious, redeeming blood of the Lord Jesus.

And He says that this is a free gift, that we are saved by grace, and not by our works. For if our works could save us, then we would surely boast, letting everyone know just how good we are. A gift, however, is something one humbly and thankfully receives, knowing he could never repay the benefactor. And this unspeakable gift transfers you from the domain of darkness, placing you once and for all into the kingdom of Christ where you receive the forgiveness of your sins and the gift of the Holy Spirit. He promises never to leave you nor forsake you. He promises to be with you when you walk through the fire. He promises to never allow the waters of life to overflow you. He promises to meet your every need in Christ Jesus. He says that no good thing will He withhold from those who walk uprightly.

Isn't it time, my dear friends, to listen to the One who gave Himself for you? Why will you refuse Him who speaks to you through His word? Don't be a fool. Give up your prideful arrogance. Cast yourself on the great Savior of sinners, the marvelous lover of your soul. Seek the Lord while He may be found. Call upon Him while He is near. Forsake your evil ways and turn to the Lord for He will abundantly pardon. Listen to Him who says, "Come to Me, all who are weary and heavy laden, and I will give you rest. Take My yoke upon you and learn from Me, for I am gentle and humble of heart and you shall find rest for your souls." With the tax gatherer in Jesus' day cry out, "God be merciful to me the sinner." Be sure of this, my friend—the great lover and Savior of your soul cannot lie! He will do what He says He will do. Come to Jesus right now. How? Simply turn from your sin and believe on the Lord Jesus Christ. He will save you. He will wash away your sin. He will give you His Holy Spirit. He will remove the wrath of God hanging like the Sword of Damocles over your head. You will find peace with God. You will find peace within yourself. He will take you to heaven when you die. He will give you a glorified body on the new earth when He comes again in glory.

The Lake of Fire: What's It Like, Who Goes There, When, and Why?

And the sea gave up the dead which were in it, and death and Hades gave up the dead which were in them; and they were judged, every one of them according to their deeds. And death and Hades were thrown into the lake of fire. This is the second death, the lake of fire. And if anyone's name was not found written in the book of life, he was thrown into the lake of fire, Revelation 21:13-15.

My friends, there can be no more sobering words in all the world than these I just read to you. They speak of unbearable and unimaginable horror. What is meant by the term "lake of fire"? Is it a locale, and if so, who goes there? Furthermore, when do they go there, and why do they go there?

Let us imagine, for the sake of argument, that you have a dear friend whom you have known since you were both in eighth grade. You have remained friends for all these many years. You attempted, numerous times over the years, to introduce your friend to the Savior, but he was always unwilling to take seriously his need for forgiveness of sins and spiritual direction in his life.

Now he has died, and you are very, very concerned about where he might be at this very moment. While we should never speculate with finality concerning a loved one who has died and who showed little interest in Christ (after all, we are not privy to his thoughts and prayers as the end drew near for him and what he might or might not have done concerning his need for Christ), nonetheless you cannot help but ask the question, "Where now is my best friend?" As I attempted to show you on Sunday night, if your friend was indeed born again to a living hope through the resurrection of Jesus Christ from the dead, then he is now experiencing joy inexpressible and full of glory. At the moment of his death his soul was separated from his body. The body went to the grave to decay, but the soul went immediately into the presence of Jesus Christ where myriads of angels, the glorified saints in heaven, the twenty-four elders, and the four living creatures are constantly singing praise to Jesus Christ, "Worthy art Thou, our Lord and our God, to receive glory and honor and power; for Thou didst create all things, and because of Thy will they existed, and were created," (Revelation 4:11). He is conscious. He knows where he is, in the presence of the Lord Jesus Christ, our resurrected and glorious judge, king, and Savior. His life which he sought to live for Jesus but which, nonetheless, was plagued with many failures due to indwelling sin and the temptations of the world, the flesh, and the devil, is now in perfect peace and rest. His soul has been made perfect and the vestiges of sin which he battled mightily throughout his entire life are now gone completely.

If however he died without ever calling on the name of the Lord Jesus Christ to be saved, then he is now in hell, a place of untold, unmitigated horror where the fire is never quenched and the worm never dies. He is conscious of his existence in hell, a place of outer darkness (completely alone, without ever seeing anyone), where there is weeping and gnashing of teeth (unbridled hostility and hatred toward the

Lord Jesus, but also unrelenting remorse at what could have been).

But as I have shown already, both heaven and hell are not the final resting place for people. Both are what theologians call "the intermediate state." The new earth, mentioned in Isaiah 65, 66, 2 Peter 3, and Revelation 20, is the final resting place for the blood bought saints of the Lord Jesus Christ. At the moment of Christ's second coming, when He shall descend from heaven with a shout, with the voice of the archangel, and the sound of a trumpet, the dead in Christ (the bodies of the redeemed which have been in the grave since death) will rise and be caught up together with the saints still alive on earth (1 Thessalonians 4:16,17). They will receive glorified bodies, like the One the Lord Jesus now has in heaven (1 Corinthians 15:42-44, 50-58). God will burn up the fallen world in which we now live, but he will restore the world to its original pristine purity and perfection which it had before the disastrous fall into sin in the Garden of Eden. The Bible calls this "the new earth." All of God's people from all ages shall live there with the Lord Jesus. There will be no sickness or death there. There will be no more mourning, grieving, crying, or pain. It appears that animals will also be there because the new earth is a restoration of all things as it was in the beginning, while Isaiah also says that the wolf and lamb shall graze together, the lion shall eat straw like an ox (Isaiah 65:25).

However there is a dreadful downside to the truth of the new earth. As heaven is the precursor to the new earth, so hell is the precursor to the lake of fire. The lake of fire is mentioned five times in the New Testament (Revelation 19:20, 20:10,14,15, 21:8).

Revelation 20:14 calls the lake of fire the second death. All people will die at least once, unless the Lord Jesus returns before some of His people have died. Those born twice, a physical birth after developing in their mother's womb for nine months, but also a supernatural birth through the regenerating work of the Holy Spirit, will die only once. But those born once, coming from their mother's womb, will die twice. The first death is when they cease to breathe. At death their souls are separated from their bodies and they go down to hell. But there is also a second death, just mentioned in the passage from Revelation 21, and John the Apostle calls that second death the lake of fire. The lake of fire is the final resting place for all the damned who have ever lived. All these people had rejected the overtures of free grace from preachers and evangelists sent out by the Lord Jesus to all the earth. They died, and then faced judgment. Being found guilty they were cast into the lake of fire where the beast and the false prophets are also.

My task here is not to go down a rabbit trail and spill much ink on giving you a detailed rationale for who, I believe, the beast and the false prophet are, but I will say that John was writing directly to Christian people suffering under the Roman Emperor around 70 A.D. So I believe the beast was the Roman Emperor Nero who, at the time, was severely persecuting the church; and the false prophet was probably a term for many false prophets living at the time who were posing as messengers from God, but who, in fact, were leading the bond servants of Christ away from Him. Revelation 19:20 tells us that the lake of fire burns with brimstone. Interestingly, if you visit today the place of Sodom and Gomorrah where God rained down fire and brimstone on those wicked cities latent with homosexual perversion, you would still be able to find brimstone, a sulfurous rock, inside a casing of lava rocks from a volcanic eruption which destroyed Sodom. All of Israel was aware of what had happened there and many had seen the effects of the eruption. These served as vivid reminders and warnings of just how dreadful the lake of fire is.

We can go further and say that the lake of fire is a place of torment, day and night, forever and ever (Revelation 20:10). The devil joins the beast and the false prophet in the lake of fire. Revelation 20:13, in referencing the Great White Throne Judgment, tells us that both death and Hades are thrown into the lake of fire. This is another way of saying that the very concept of death will be forever cast from the existence of God's blood bought people, because it has been removed from the earth and placed in the place of death. And Hades was the resting place of all the dead in Old Testament times. Hades was not clearly marked as heaven or hell in the Old Testament. It was simply the place where the dead rested until the resurrection of all things. But this holding place for death will also no longer be necessary.

And we are told in Revelation 20:15 that not only the false prophet, the beast, the devil, and death and Hades are thrown into the lake of fire which burns with brimstone, but also any person whose name is not found written in the Lamb's book of life. John enlarges on the identity of those who names are not found in the book of life. He says, "But for the cowardly and unbelieving and abominable and murderers and immoral persons and sorcerers and idolaters and all liars, their part is in the lake that burns with fire and brimstone, which is the second death."

So to summarize, the lake of fire is the final resting place of all the damned angels, false prophets, leaders, and wicked, vile people who have ever lived. It is far worse than hell ever could be. In fact we might say with great confidence that everyone in hell this very moment would give everything they ever had to stay there another one million years.

Why? Why would anyone ever prefer hell over some other place? Because all the damned sinners in hell dread "that day." And what is "that day?" It is the judgment day, the day in which every unbeliever stands before the tribunal of God's righteous judgment where He metes out to His enemies exactly what they deserve. Revelation 20:12 states it this way, "And I saw the dead, the great and the small, standing before the throne, and books were opened; and another book was opened, which is the book of life; and the dead were judged from the things which were written in the books, according to their deeds." What does this mean, "books were opened; and another book was opened, which is the book of life?" The book of life refers to the book where the names of God's people, redeemed by the blood of Christ, are recorded. In Jesus' letter to the church at Sardis He says that those who overcome will thus be clothed in white garments and He promises never to erase their names from the book of life (Revelation 3:5). When the seventy returned from preaching and casting out demons Jesus told them not to rejoice because spirits were subject to them, but because their names are recorded in heaven (Luke 10:20). These passages are telling us that God knows exactly those who are His. He calls them all by name, like a shepherd calls his sheep, and they all know his voice and they follow him.

But the "books" are a different matter. They refer to all who are outside of Christ and this speaks of judgment. Revelation 20:12 says that they are all judged according to their deeds. My friends, can there be anything more frightening than to have every single thing you have ever done evaluated by the King of Glory, the Holy and Majestic One, who by no means leaves the guilty unpunished? Actually this judgment is in three different ways. First of all is the judgment of actions. Revelation 20:12 speaks clearly of this but Jesus says something similar in Matthew 16:27, "For the Son of Man is going to come in the glory of His Father with His angels; and will then recompense every man according to his deeds."

So, at the return of the Lord Jesus, every unbeliever will stand before Jesus Christ, the great Judge of all the earth, and give account of every thing they have done. Each person will have the deeds which he did in his life paraded before the Righteous Judge, the Lord Jesus Christ. The standard of measure will be the pure and undefiled Law of God. Did this deed, did that deed measure up to God's standard of perfection? But wait, the Righteous Judge goes further. He will examine the things which were not done, but which should have been done, like the time the person should have helped the little woman across the street, like the time he should have given food to a poor person. The deeds will be found lacking in the balance and the person will know exactly how far short he has fallen of God's perfect standard.

How do you think you will fare, my friends, when you stand before the Lord Jesus and give account of every deed you have done, of every deed you should have done, but did not do?

It gets worse, for not only are one's deeds judged, but also one's thoughts as well. The Apostle Paul in Romans 2:14-16, in referencing the Gentiles who do not have the advantage of having the Law as the Jews do, lays down this vital and staggering truth. "For when Gentiles who do not have the Law do instinctively the things of the Law, these, not having the Law, are a law to themselves, in that they show the work of the Law written in their hearts, their conscience bearing witness, and their thoughts alternately accusing or else defending them, on the day when, according to my gospel, God will judge the secrets of men through Christ Jesus."

Paul is saying that though the Jews had the advantage of having the Old Testament Law while the Gentiles were disadvantaged in not having the Law, nonetheless, if Gentiles could keep the Law then they could be saved. Of course, they could not keep the Law any better than the Jews or anyone else, for that matter. So ultimately their thoughts are accusing them, just as the thoughts of the Jews accuse them. They both know they fail to keep the Law of God, and not only do their own consciences judge them, but God will also judge their thoughts through the Lord Jesus Christ.

So, on the day of the Great White Throne Judgment every unbeliever will stand before the Lord Jesus and give account of every thought they ever had. God will bring before the unbeliever every blasphemous, lascivious, wicked, vile, idolatrous, angry, embittered, unforgiving thought they have ever had.

How do you think you will do when you stand before God, and every thought you have ever had will be judged by the pure, holy, undefiled, sovereign Creator, Sustainer, and Judge?

But wait, there is one more detail you need to have clearly set in your mind. Not only will your deeds and thoughts be judged, but also your words will be judged by the One whose eyes are a flame of fire, whose name is Holy, Holy, Holy. Jesus says, "The good man out of the good treasure brings forth what is good; and the evil man out of his evil treasure brings forth what is evil. And I say to you, every careless word that men shall speak, they shall render account for in the day of judgment. For by your words you shall be justified, and by your words you shall be condemned," (Matthew 12:35-37.

We should ever bless and thank our God. Why? Because our Lord Jesus Christ, the One who was delivered over because of our transgressions, and was raised again from the dead for our justification, has once and for all taken our sins from us, having them nailed to the cross. The unbeliever, on the other hand, has no such grace in his life. His every careless word, whether blasphemous, perverse, arrogant, or prideful is being recorded by the Lord Jesus, and He will judge these people for every careless, lascivious word they utter.

How are you doing with this truth, my dear friend? If indeed God marks or records our iniquity, then none of us can stand.

So, as God judges the unbeliever's thoughts, words, and actions, he will be unable to open his own mouth to make his defense (Romans 3:19). He will be speechless. I have noticed on several occasions when people are struck with fear they are speechless. I remember a friend telling me that many years, before the 9/11 terrorist attack, he was on a plane to Africa when a terrorist had the pilot by the throat and was seeking to remove him from the cockpit. The plane was violently rocking back and forth as it was nose diving toward the African desert. For the first several minutes, as this was unfolding, no one on the plane made a sound. They were dumb struck at the real possibility of their deaths. Finally my friend and another took care of the terrorist and the plane later landed safely in Nairobi.

The greatest fear anyone could possibly have is to stand before Almighty God as their thoughts, words, and actions are displayed before the Holy gaze of the Sovereign Judge of all things.

It is at this point that God the Father makes His just judgment and pronouncement on every condemned sinner in the world, a judgment they knew was coming but dreaded moment by moment as the time of their pronounced day of reckoning drew near. Jesus will say to them, "Depart from Me, accursed ones, into the eternal fire which has been prepared for the devil and his angels," (Matthew 25:41). At that very moment each one pronounced "guilty" will be cast into the lake of fire, the second death.

It is at this point, that every condemned sinner will know with no uncertainty that he is receiving exactly the punishment he deserves. The lake of fire and the second death is the most sobering of all realities. Are you, my friends, ready to meet God?

But at this juncture you may ask, "Wait a minute. Isn't this way over the top? God is a God of mercy and grace. He delights in forgiveness and lovingkindness. He loves everyone. How then can you say that He will cast people into the lake of fire? This does not seem just."

The reason you and so many people balk at these words of eternal wrath and condemnation is because you do not readily acknowledge the notion that the penalty meted must equal the weight of the crime committed. God is just. He is incapable of denying His justice. People must be given what is due them. Paul says the wages of sin is death (Romans 6:23a). A grown son who has lived with his parents and who has been given the very best in clothing, food, education, and love; but who decides to beat his parents to death with a baseball bat while they are sleeping, is guilty of a heinous crime. He deserves death for his wicked, premeditated act of murder.

However a teen aged boy who has no father, who lives in a ghetto, who is caring for his very sick mother, and who consequently had to drop out of school, and who steals a few frozen food meals from the local grocery store, should not be tried, convicted, and sentenced to many years in prison for his petty theft. The punishment must fit the crime.

The same is true with God's justice. So when we find repeatedly in the Bible that God will by no means leave the guilty unpunished, that unbelievers who have repeatedly rejected the overtures of free grace offered to every sinner everywhere in the world, will be cast into the lake of fire, we should not be shocked. To deny this necessity is to deny two vital and non-negotiable truths. First, God is absolutely, without equivocation, Holy. There is not the slightest taint or vestige of sin in Him in anyway. We are called to be holy as God is holy, and none us come even close to this reality. Jesus tells us that we must be perfect, even as our Heavenly Father is perfect. The unbeliever stands naked before the tribunal of God's just justice. He receives the justice he deserves. The believer, on the other hand, stands clothed in the righteousness of Jesus Christ. His sins, though many, are not counted against him. Though his sins were as scarlet, they are made whiter than snow. Though they were red like crimson, they are white like wool. Why? How, can this be true? Because the believer's sins were placed on Christ at the cross. "Greater is He who is in us, than he who is in the world," (1 John 4:4).

So, who will be cast into the lake of fire? Every unbeliever will go there. When? On the day of judgment.

My friends, the lake of fire, the second death, is far worse than anyone can possibly imagine or contemplate. It is a sea without a shore. A man stranded in the ocean has high hopes that he can somehow reach land, if he can only hang on a little while longer. He wills himself to stay alive because he is hoping for the best. The lake of fire, however, has no land on which anyone could go for rest or refuge. This is the height of despair, fear, and hopelessness. Those in the lake of fire are burning but not consumed, grieving but not comforted, striving for rest but never able to reach it, seeking for divine favor but always being the recipients of divine wrath.

I wish I could tell you that due to God's mercy, those in hell or the lake of fire will eventually be annihilated, but there is no indication in the Bible that this will happen. Revelation 20:10 says that those in the lake of fire will be tormented day and night forever and ever. Some have taught that God, in His mercy, will eventually annihilate every soul in the lake of fire. That is, they will simply cease to exist and no longer suffer torment away from the presence of the Lord and the glory of His power. But the lake of fire is forever. There is no end to the suffering, despair, and sorrow for the damned. The tears of remorse for rejecting Christ will ever flow. The anguish of "what might have been if only I had come to Christ" will never disappear.

What shall you do, my friends? I know you say you do not really believe it can be all that bad, even if hell and the lake of fire do, in fact, exist. But you know this truth because you have eternity written on your heart. You know the Bible is right when it says that it is appointed for men to die once, and then comes the judgment. You say you do not believe that, but deep in your heart, you know this is true.

What then, must you? How can you escape hell and the lake of fire? How can you know intimately and personally the Lord Jesus Christ, the great and marvelous lover of your soul?

I do not seek to denigrate anyone nor their religion. People are certainly free to believe whatever they wish. I always champion that right. However, to say this does not mean that all faith systems are equal. It is true that religion has often been an opiate of the people. It has led millions into superstition and genocide, but that about which the writer to the Hebrews speaks is not the same thing as other religions. Christianity is totally unique. If religion is man's effort to reach up to God, then Christianity is God's great act of condescension, ripping open heaven, coming into the world as a baby born in a manger, born in obscurity and poverty, living perfectly, proclaiming the kingdom of God by His life, words, actions, and death, proving that He has purchased the redemption of His people by being raised from the dead and ascending to His Father's right hand.

And now you must stop neglecting this great salvation being offered to you. Enough is enough. It is sheer madness, my friend, to not consider the sure and certain ending of your life. You will die, and then comes the judgment. You will stand before God and give an account of all you have said, thought, and done. Do you feel good about your chances to pass the perfect gaze of unmitigated holiness? Where will you go when you die? Contrary to what so many believe, you will not simply die and cease to exist. You have a soul that will never die. You will not merely return to the dust from which you came. Deep down in your heart you know what I am saying is true. That's because God has written eternity on your heart.

You will not get a second chance in purgatory. There is no such place. God has given you time to repent during your lifetime, and thus far you have refused to heed His cry. Furthermore, you will not come back from the dead as some other person. There is no such thing as reincarnation. These are all lies of the devil to blind you to eternal verities, to drug you, as it were, so that you will live and die in your spiritual stupor.

Do not neglect this glorious, marvelous, and majestic salvation any longer. Stop your drifting. Come to Jesus right now. What does it mean to come to Jesus? By this I don't mean a mere religious life of church going, though this is important. I don't mean an emotional decision wrought by sheer terror at the thought of dying. But by this I do mean coming to grips with your mortality, your lack of true spirituality, the just condemnation for your sins under which you are now living. I mean seeing that you have offended a holy God, that Jesus is your only hope of eternal salvation, that you are willing to acknowledge your sinful rebellion against Him, that you are willing to hate and forsake your sin, that you ask God to save you by the death and resurrection of the Lord Jesus Christ. By this I mean you trust only in who Jesus is and what He did on the cross. You must see that you have nothing to offer Him, that your righteousness is like a menstrual cloth before Him. You must believe that Jesus' death and resurrection is the full payment and satisfaction of God for your sins. It means you say to God, "Be merciful to me, the sinner." It means that you are able to say about yourself with Paul the Apostle, "I am the foremost of sinners."

You must flee from your sins and call on the name of the Lord Jesus Christ to save you. How do you do so? You must say, "God, please be merciful to me, a great sinner." If you are hit by shrapnel from a suicide bomber and are bleeding out, then you know you are in a desperate situation. You will not casually ask for help. You will do all you can to alert people to your perilous condition. You will cry out loudly for help. And so it is with those whom the Holy Spirit has convicted. This is no casual matter. This is eternal life and death hanging in the balance. In other words, you must surrender yourself totally to Jesus. If you do so, then He promises that He will give you a new heart that loves God and hates sin. He will wash away all your sin and filth, its inexorable guilt and shame, removing the just condemnation coming upon you from the Holy One who will by no means leave the guilty unpunished. And you must simply trust what Jesus did on the cross, in His death and in His resurrection. You must believe that His death alone pays the penalty for your sins. You cannot do anything to earn your forgiveness. It is a sheer act of God's grace and mercy. You will also receive the gift of the Holy Spirit who will work constantly to strengthen you to deny sin, and to walk in obedience to God's word. Will you flee to Jesus? What is keeping you from Him? Believe on Him today!

Are you willing to do so my friend? It matters not how long you have been away from God. It matters not how sinfully you have lived over these many years. It matters not how dreadfully you have hurt others, though surely you will want to make restitution to those whom you have hurt by confessing your sins to them and asking for their forgiveness. It matters not that the consequences of your sin are so profound and far reaching that you can never unravel the deceit and hardship you have caused others. Jesus is ready, willing, and able to save you right this very moment. Turn from your sin, my friend, and believe on Jesus Christ to save you. You will find Him to be all that He promises. You will know His peace, love, guidance, and provision all your days. And when you close your eyes in death, you will see grandeur and majesty beyond comprehension. Only Jesus can save you, and He can do so right now!

Appendix

What follows are the words of a gospel tract I have written and use in my open air preaching ministry.

And if anyone's name was not found written in the book of life, he was thrown into the lake of fire, Revelation 20:15.

The Lake of Fire: What's It Like, Who Goes There, and Why?

Since people everywhere die daily and since you have no guarantee whatsoever that you will live past today, should you not contemplate, along with everyone else, the end for all the damned who have ever lived in this world? Can there be any more sobering reality than what we read in the verse noted above? And should you not, my dear friend, contemplate your own eternal existence after your earthly demise? Read this with fear and trembling. I write without the slightest equivocation. If you die without being a Christian, without being born again through the regenerating work of the Holy Spirit, if you never gain the life of God in your soul, then upon your death your soul will immediately go to hell, a place of conscious, eternal torment, where the fire is never quenched and the worm never dies. As bad as hell is, however, you would give everything you have, to stay there in hell for a million years.

Why? Because those now in hell know what you will know when you transition to there. They fear more than anything "that day." And what is "that day"? It is the great white throne judgment, because there, on the day of Christ's return, all the dead, unsaved sinners who have ever lived, great and small, will stand before God and give account of the deeds they have done, according to the things written in the book. Know this too, the resurrection of Jesus Christ is a two-edged sword. Paul says that because Jesus Christ has been raised from the dead, He is the first fruits of those who are asleep (1 Corinthians 15:20). Paul wonderfully and vividly lays out the case for glorified bodies for the saints. At the last trumpet, the dead will be raised imperishable. However, the reuniting of body and soul on the new earth for believers is also true of unbelievers at the great white throne judgment. Daniel says, "Many of those who sleep in the dust of the ground will awake, these to everlasting life; but the others to disgrace and everlasting contempt," (Daniel 12:2). Jesus tells us not to fear man who can kill the body. Rather we are to fear God who can destroy both the body and soul in hell (Matthew 10:28). And the parable of the rich man in hell makes clear that he possessed a body. He was asking Lazarus to place a drop of water on his tongue to quench his thirst (Luke 16:24). It is one thing to suffer in one's own soul in hell. It is quite another to suffer in body and soul in the final judgment.

So, if you are a hell bound sinner, why should you fear the great white throne judgment more than hell itself? Because you, and every other unbeliever, will stand, body and soul, before King Jesus to witness the charges against you and them. As you stand, by yourself, before the thrice Holy God, the jealous and avenging God, who will by no means leave the guilty unpunished, your thoughts will be judged (Romans 2:16). Jesus will summon every thought you ever had

—your lusts, anger, bitterness, bigotry, jealousy, envy —and place them alongside His holy law. You will be speechless (Romans 3:19). You will have no defense. You are doomed and you know it. Then your words will be summoned, because Jesus said that every careless word will be judged (Matthew 12:36). All those harsh, foul, sensual, vile, blasphemous, lying, manipulating, degrading words you spoke throughout your life will be placed alongside the purity of the One with whom we all must give an account. No defense there either. Finally, your every action will be judged (2 Corinthians 5:10, Revelation 20:12, Matthew 16:27). All of the millions of times you disobeyed God, in what we might call small or large ways, will be evaluated in light of His perfect law. Every jealous, selfish, licentious, sensual, idolatrous act you ever did, will be judged by the One whose eyes are a flaming fire, whose feet are like bronze made to glow in a furnace. Not only your sins of commission, but perhaps even more dreadfully, your sins of omission will be judged. You will remember the times you passed by a needy man on the street and did nothing to help him. You will remember the multitudinous times you neglected to care for your spouse, children, parents, or close friends. You will remember the times you hated instead of loved your enemy. You will also be unable to make a defense before God for your actions.

With all of this evidence now displayed before you and the Holy One, you will hear those words you knew were coming but have dreaded the entire time you were in hell, the most awful words which could ever be uttered, "Depart from Me, you accursed one, into the eternal fire which has been prepared for the devil and his angels," (Matthew 25:41). And as you are being led from the great white throne of God to be cast into the lake of fire, you will know for certain, without the slightest equivocation, that you are receiving the exact judgment you deserve.

The lake of fire is the second death. Many have noted that those who are born once, will die twice; and those who are born twice will die once. And what will you do in the lake of fire? Presumably the same thing you have been doing in hell from the moment you arrived there, but now, due to the union of body and soul, the pain, horror, and awareness will be infinitely magnified. As in hell, there will be weeping or wailing along with the gnashing of teeth. I have heard the anguish and grief of unmitigated wailing coming from one who has suddenly lost a child or a spouse. Perhaps you have also. It is terrible. The wailing in the lake of fire will be infinitely worse. Every sense will be heightened there. Though you are alone in darkness, you nonetheless will hear the hopeless wailing of the damned. With your eyes which on earth looked at pornography or read blasphemous books denying the Christ whom you have always hated, you will look on untold, unimaginable horror. With your ears which listened to wicked jokes and took in perverse, godless, licentious ideas, you will now hear the cries of the condemned. They beg for mercy but there is none forthcoming. With your mouth, which uttered blasphemous, vile, crude, demeaning speech, you will curse God and His servants with loud voices of contempt, hatred, and sorrow. With your hands, which were engaged in all manner of creative sinning, building kingdoms for yourself which you used to oppress other people, they will now reach up to heaven, begging for a touch from the God whom you rejected, but there is no reciprocation from the Holy

One. Your feet, which were swift to run to the shedding of innocent blood and to take you to places of sensual delight and debauchery, will then seek to run for refuge, but they will be like feet stuck in cement. There is no deliverance from judgment. There is no hope. You are lost in a most dreadful judgment. There is no mercy in the lake of fire.

Do you think this is over the top? My friend, I am so completely limited in my ability to communicate to you the horrors of hell and the lake of fire. It is infinitely worse than I am able to portray to you.

You will have no second chance after you die. You must come to Jesus in this life or you will not come at all. And can you be so sure that you will live past today? Don't you know people who one day seemed to be in picture perfect health, and the next day were dead! The devil's great ploy is to tell you that you have plenty of time to get religion. "Don't worry," he says, "about that now. Live it up, then maybe when you are old and tired and have nothing better to do, you can become a Christian." But if you persist as you are, then surely you will die in your sins, be cast into hell, and eventually end up in the lake of fire. Then, my friend, what will you do? Paul the Apostle said, "Today is the day of salvation." Jesus said, "Come to Me all who are weary and heavy laden, I will give you rest." He also said, "Truly, truly I say to you, he who believes on Me has eternal life." He said to the thief on the cross who had believed on Him, "Today you will be with Me in paradise." Isaiah says, "Seek the Lord while He may be found. Call upon Him while He is near." If you believe on the Lord Jesus, He promises to forgive all your sins, to give you His righteousness and holiness, to hear your prayers, and to take you to heaven when you die. Where else can you go for relief from sin, hell, and the second death? Why die in your sins? There is no need. Run to Jesus! He is ready and willing to save you right now.

And if Jesus has saved you, why not bow reverently this very moment and thank Him for saving your soul and delivering you from hell fire? It matters not one bit your lot in life, your financial or professional status or accomplishments. Rejoice, my friend, that your name is written in the Lamb's book of life.

The Scripture is very clear, my friend, "Everyone who calls on the name of the Lord will be saved," (Romans 10:13). It also says that if you confess with your lips that Jesus is Lord and believe in your heart that God has raised Him from the dead you will be saved. For man believes with his heart and so is justified and confesses with his lips and so is saved, (Romans 10:9,10).

Call on Him right now. Say to Him, "God, please me merciful to me, a sinner." If you see your great need and call on Jesus then He will forgive you, cleanse you, empower you by the Holy Spirit, take out your rebellious heart which loves sin and hates God, and give you His heart which loves God and hates sin.

Do not delay. Call on Him now. Today is the day of salvation. There is no more important decision you will ever make.

Made in the USA
Lexington, KY
13 February 2019